SPOT REMOVER

TREATING SKIN PIGMENTATION FOR GOOD
WRITTEN BY, ANNASTAZIA UNCE, L.E.

D1825467

For King and Ameera. Everything I do is for you guys. The future is in your hands!
-Love Mommy <3

SPOT REMOVER
TREATING SKIN PIGMENTATION FOR GOOD

WRITTEN BY, ANNASTAZIA UNCE

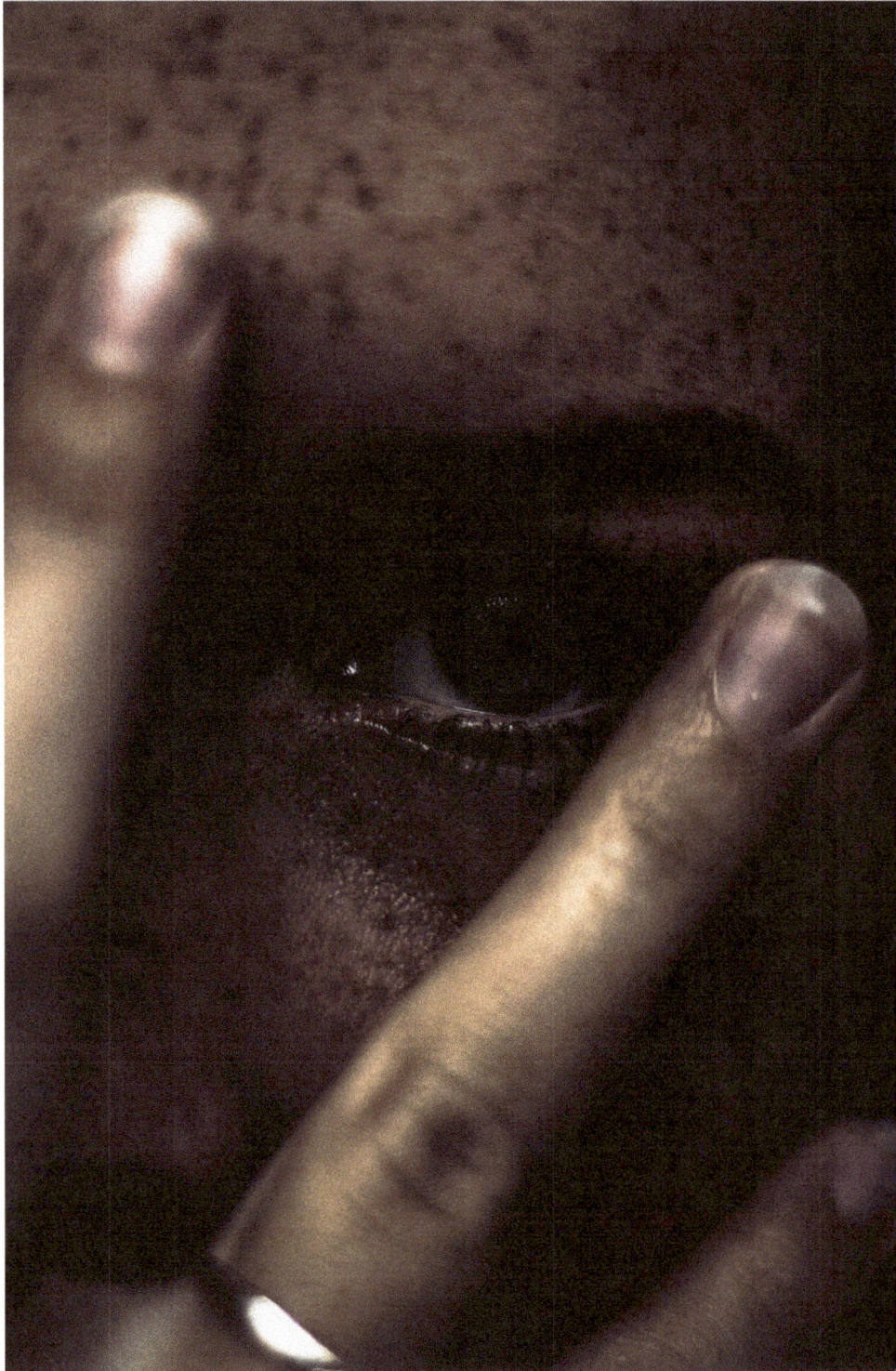

Introduction

So many people ask me what my client's number one skin concerns are, and my answer is more than always hyperpigmentation. Even though it affects men and women equally the majority of my clients and women, and having dark spots has a way of really damaging anyone's self-esteem. It's tough to step out into the world and feel confident when you know your face is covered in dark spots. It breaks my heart the most to see a client that comes in for a consultation and every day they tell me they never leave the house without makeup, or immediately after a facial the first thing they do is put on that mask of makeup to protect themselves. You all spoke, and I listened. I wrote this book with the purpose to help you fade your hyperpigmentation and keep it away for good.

How to use this book
This book is broken into two main sections. The first section is the "Professional" section; I'll discuss the procedures and steps you need to follow with a professional aesthetician or dermatologist. The second section of this book is the "Homecare" second. In this section, you will learn about the procedures that you need to follow at home as well as continue with your professional treatments to treat your skin and keep your dark spots away.

You should always keep in mind that getting rid of hyperpigmentation is a marathon, not a sprint. It can be a long road to fading your dark spots because hyperpigmentation goes so deep into the various layers of the skin. Processes can take time to penetrate deeply and stop the process that creates hyperpigmentation. Stick to the steps in this book like glue and stay consistent that's the key to getting the results that you want. Stay encouraged and hang in there honey!

What is Hyperpigmentation?

Hyperpigmentation is the presence of excess melanin (pigment) through melanogenesis. Melanogenesis is the process by which pigment is produced or overproduced in the skin.

There are 3 common causes of hyperpigmentation:

1. Sun/UV Induced - Overexposure to the sun and tanning beds without proper sun protection can cause hyperpigmentation. This form of hyperpigmentation usually presents itself as diffused spots or dark patches that evenly distributed around the face.

2. Hormone-Induced/Melasma - This pigmentation is caused by any change in hormones. Common causes of hormone fluctuations are pregnancy, contraceptives, thyroid disorders, and certain hormone therapies. This kind of hyperpigmentation presents itself as symmetrical patches on the cheeks, jawline, and forehead.

3. Post-inflammatory Hyperpigmentation - PIH is a pigment that is deposited when the skin experiences any kind of trauma, irritation, or abrasion. Most common causes are acne lesions, chronic picking, and chemical burns.

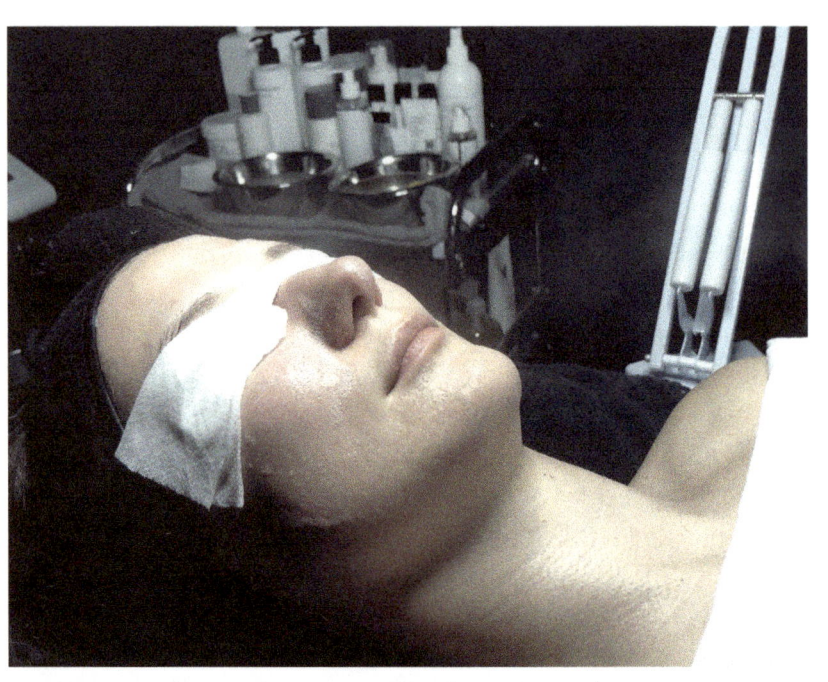

Professional Treatments

Working with a licensed skincare professional will take your skincare journey to the next level. Any dedicated professional will have pursued a path to gaining an education. An esthetician will be able to dive into your life and dissect the causes and solutions to many of your skin woes. As a professional I look at everything in a consultation, areas like diet, skincare products, sleep habits, and stress levels. Pinpointing the problem areas and fashioning the regimen to correct it is essential to ditching the hyperpigmentation.

Finding your Professional

How should you go about finding a skincare professional that will best assist you in reaching your skin goals? You can approach this task similarly to how you would for hiring an employee. You'll want to know they're working history, accomplishments, and how long have they been in the industry? But, years in the industry doesn't always equal experience or expertise, so asking what kind of continuing educations classes or certifications they have is also a good place to start. You can ask to see if they have any before and after pictures is a good way to see some of their clients' success stories. Go into this interview process with an open mind and no preconceived notions yet still keep the goal of finding answers in the forefront. If you're too pushy, it's easy to come off condescending or rude. You don't want to be labeled as the "difficult" client, and nothing can turn off a practitioner quicker than an overly opinionated client. Your entering into a relationship, a partnership if you will, so keep it pleasant. You'll be working together for a long time.

Step One: Consultation

First thing, if the spa your planning on attending doesn't offer a consultation before your first service, don't bother going. Beforehand even touch your skin learning about your and your skin. It's a great idea to bring any products and medications your currently using into your consultation. Having this handy will help your technician identify sensitivities and conflicting ingredients. Secondly, be honest! You'll be asked a lot of probing questions. Even questions like how often you poop! But answer honestly, your answers could mean the difference between a great service with amazing results or walking home with a rash and permanent scarring. After this conversation, you should be able to identify your skin type, the products that harming your skin and what the replacement product should be, the frequency of your treatments, and any lifestyle changes.

Step Two: First Facial

The first facial should be your esthetician's initial introduction to your skin. Treatments should be mild and geared towards moisturizing and repairing any damage caused to your skins natural barrier, after your initial facial is when your esthetician will recommend a home-care routine, products, then present they're plain for fading your dark spots. Having your esthetician focus on exfoliating with an enzyme-based exfoliate to gently dissolve dead skin cells is the best way to gage the reaction of your skin level and remove buildup at the same time.

In skin care, we use protein-degrading enzymes found mostly in plants, fruits, and vegetables. Enzymes break down the bonds between cells and allow them to shed naturally. An esthetician can use enzymes alone or with the aid of acids or scrubs. Most are so gently they're used on all skin types and. Common enzymes are:

1. Pineapple
2. Papaya
3. Cherry
4. Grape
5. Pumpkin

Step Three: The Plan

Below I've recommended a general plan to follow with your professional to fade your hyperpigmentation. Be mindful that some steps may vary from person to person since everyone skin is different, and what might one work for one might not work for another. But the common factor for everyone is consistency. These programs WILL cost you money honey, but if you're serious about your skin goals, you can make it work. And most estheticians have packages to encourage clients to stay consistent, and these packages may offer a bit of discount as a reward for committing.

6 MONTH PLAN

- 2 weeks from your first facial schedule a low percentage chemical peel.

- Continue with treatments every 2 weeks for 12 weeks, while gradually increasing the peel percentage.

- After 3 months for bi-monthly peels reduces treatments to once a month.

- Monthly treatments can be enzyme or peel based

exfoliating treatments.

- Adding microdermabrasion or hydrodermabrasion to monthly facials will enhance brightening effects.

- Follow your professionals At-home product regimen recommendations.

Homecare Treatments

When explaining the relationship between Professional treatments and a Homecare routine, I usually compare them to visiting a healthcare physician. Every year you visit your doctor for a physical then your physician may write you a prescription or put you on a treatments plan. When it comes to skincare, out regular facials are the check-up, and your Homecare is your medication. Both are designed to keep you healthy and to maintain or enhance the results of your treatment. Any client that has regular facials but doesn't purchase and use products will never fully achieve the results that they're hoping for so don't expect your esthetician or dermatologist to do all the heavy lifting without you holding up your end of the bargain. Following a routine at home is paramount for fading dark spots and hyperpigmentation because they are so stubborn. As I've stated before, staying persistent and not giving up will get you the desired results. Key products like a cleanser, exfoliant, and SPF should be included in your regimen. Also, a lightening agent has to be added to this routine for the actualization of "spot free" skin to become real.

AHA and BHA
Alpha Hydroxy Acid and Beta Hydroxy Acid work miracles for the skin. They are exfoliants that are scientifically derived from natural ingredients to remove skin cells. AHAs work on the skin's surface by loosening the bond between cells allowing them to shed quickly. AHAs are water-soluble making them ideal for normal to dry skin types and best for skin with hyperpigmentation caused by sun damage. The most common AHA ingredients are Glycolic Acid (derived

for sugar cane) and Lactic acid (derived for milk). BHAs work both on the surface of the skin and inside the pores. BHAs are oil-soluble making them ideal for oily and acne-prone skin types since oil attracts oil its great for unclogging pores and keeping dark spot causing breakouts away.

Naturally Derived Lighteners
Many lighteners are very effective at fading dark spots and hyperpigmentation; some also have melanin suppressing properties. Naturally derived lighteners have been scientifically isolated and extracted to be used alone or in skincare products. Exfoliating and lighteners go hand and hand when it comes to correcting dark spots. Without having a product in place to fade and suppress the discoloration will only return. It is essential to use the lighteners consistently AM and PM along with an SPF of 30 or higher. Prolonged use of natural lighteners are safe, but sun-sensitivity can occur, so if you're going to be in direct sunlight wear a hat. The most common lighteners are:

Kojic acid- Derived from fungi, more specifically the Koji mushroom from Japan.
Arbutin- Derived from the Bearberry Plant. Is an excellent alternative to Hydroquinone.
Azelaic Acid- Azelaic acid is a friendly acid derived from barley, wheat, and rye. Also unclogs pores and reduces sensitivity.
Mandelic Acid- Mandelic acid is extracted from bitter almonds, and its name comes from the German word "Mandel" for almond. Safe enough for pregnant and nursing women.
Licorice Root- The most

soothing of the lighteners. Licorice root is good for people with skin disorders and sun damage.

Retinol
Retinol is the fix all miracle ingredient! Retinol is a concentration of Vitamin A that's also available in a prescription called "Retin-A." Retinol corrects acne, diminishes wrinkles, and of course, fades hyperpigmentation. Its only downside is it makes the skin very sensitive very quickly by thinning the top layer of the skin, or the epidermis. Retinol should only be used at night and should be introduced into you regimen gradually then increased to every other night. Photo-sensitivity is guaranteed with retinol so its best not to wear it during the day and to always protect yourself from the sun. Reduce the number of nights that you use retinol if you notice redness or irritation.

Hydroquinone
Hydroquinone is a controversial skin brightener that is by far the best at fading hyperpigmentation. Its banned in many other countries due to its incorrect use. When used excessively on the skin, skin can become blue or black in color, but these are extreme cases of excessive application. Using hydroquinone with proper supervision by a licensed professional hydroquinone can be very effective at fading dark spots quickly.
I recommend the "3 months on and the 3 months off" method. Use the hydroquinone serum AM and PM for 3 months with SPF to quickly clear

the skin, then stop. For the next 3 months use a natural lightener to maintain the results. After this cycle, you can reassess your skin's condition to decide with you want to continue another cycle. While using the hydroquinone always wear sunscreen and protect yourself from the sun. Photo-sensitivity is very common with continued use, so it's important not to go over 3 months of use. If you're using the hydroquinone while on your facial treatment plan stop all lighteners, AHAs, BHAs, and other exfoliants 1 week before treatment.

Recommended Homecare Regimen *(In order of application)*

Double Cleanse
Cleanse your skin twice with a cleanser designed for your skin type. Many people can't believe the benefits of cleansing twice. Wash once to remove dirt and debris, then cleanse a second time to let the ingredients on the cleanser do their work. You'll be shocked by the results when you begin doing this.

Exfoliate
You should exfoliate your skin 2-3 times per week. Avoid over exfoliating, because it can lead to sensitivity, excessive oiliness, excessive dryness, breakout, or flaking. If you experience any of these symptoms reduce the number of times you exfoliate.

Toner

Toner is designed to rebalance your skins pH level and to hydrate the skin. It should never burn or sting like most astringents. Astringents like Sea Breeze and Witch Hazel are often confused as toners, but they dry out the skin and zap your skin's hydration. Spray toner liberally so your skin can "drink" in the hydration.

Serum
Serums are the medicine for your skin they deliver a concentrated amount of ingredients into the skin. Its molecular structure is so small that it can be quickly absorbed into the skin. The serum step is best to apply natural brighteners, retinol, AHAs, and BHAs.

Moisturizer and SPF
Moisturizer should be formulated for your specific skin type. Choose gels for oily skin, creams for dry skin, and gel-cream hybrids for everything in-between. I find that clients skip the moisturizing step or use the incorrect moisturizer, which leads to breakouts. SPF 30 or higher should be worn everyday no exceptions.

Believe it or not, this whole regimen takes only 5 mins.

About the Author

Annastazia Unce is a licensed Maryland esthetician and beauty educator with 9 years in the beauty industry. She has a passion for corrective skincare and educating men and women on proper skincare practices for the improvement of their skin. Annastazia is also an author who's best known for her eBook, "Ingredients to Run From: Skincare Products That Do Harm." She's appeared on ABC7 Good Morning Washington, The Gettin' Grown Podcast, Radio 95.9FM, DC Radio 96.3HD4, as well as various appearances in the Washington D.C. area. Her approachable personality, expertise, and public speaking experience makes her the ideal choice to participate in wellness, beauty, and entrepreneurship speaking engagements.

Visit www.KimeeraSpa.com to download "Ingredients to Run From: Skincare Products That Do Harm." This highly informative book tells clients all about skincare products that we've been told are great for our skin, but usually wreak havoc on our skin, then learn what the healthy alternatives are. Also, shop my Skincare Shopping List. This list lays out skincare products by skin type, then list the ingredients that will best work with your specific skin type.

Lightning Source UK Ltd.
Milton Keynes UK
UKHW020351091019
351230UK00007B/351/P